LOST SONGS OF THE WITHLACOOCHEE

poetry

Frederick Kirwin

Apollo Books

ISBN-13: 979-8994151600

Cover photograph: iStock.com/sdbower

Dedicated

to

Jesse Kissinger Webb

On the day of your long-remembered death,

there were no songs of fire, necessity, or depth,

no hymns to the Sun, Moon or greater Cosmos,

no chants to the Unknown, the Known, or even Apollo.

No prayers were offered to a Messiah of Virgin Birth,

and no tears of grief fell onto the receptive earth,

and no sighs of acceptance were felt by me.

Only a cold, dark stare came from my eyes in a silent plea,

and an unheard curse was hurled on high

at those Gods dwelling in the far-off sky,

for you were gone and nevermore would be mine,

and your dreaded going has touched me so

in a place too deep for tears to flow.

Only a groan from the Chambers of Regret

echoes out of my soul at sunset.

Frederick Kirwin

O Belovèd, I remember the day we met

in the Garden of Blood-Red Sunsets.

I remember the river where we swam naked

under the voluptuous Sun, radiant and sacred.

I can still see your astonishing body

with its rippling splendor in a muscular rhapsody

and feel the overwhelming amplitude of your soul

and hear the melodious accents that told

of southern charm and seduction and *bon esprit*.

I remember your *joie de vivre* and your love of me.

Frederick Kirwin

You would have loved the river today

with its immaculate waters and fish at play.

You would have thrilled at the symphonic sky

with its crescendoing thunder and birds on high

and its tympanic clouds towering up from the land.

And you would have held my hand

as we sang our way downriver to the distant strand,

wishing the river never to end in the soft, white sand.

Ah, such were you and I, my dearly belovèd,

on those days of lyrical lovemaking

sailing down the River of Adolescent Awakening.

Frederick Kirwin

I see you standing on the edge of the boat

as we floated our way down to the coast.

You were looking up at the Sun with your eyes closed,

mouthing truths into that glorious day of love and repose.

Is it a remembrance I misrecall

or a vision come back to haunt me this Fall

on this dazzling day of autumnal Sun

as I sail down the Withlacoochee, alone and undone?

Frederick Kirwin

As you lay dying in that field of heliotropic flowers,

I said a prayer to the Celestial Powers,

and whether I believed in all or none mattered not at all,

for the prayer I prayed was not answered by one or all,

and you died, not a quiet death at my side,

nor one of comprehending life,

nor recognizing those whom you once idolized,

but a death of agony and a cursing of the light,

and I left the Garden of Diminishing Delight,

seeing nothing,

beyond suffering,

beyond grief,

beyond expecting any relief,

beyond believing in the known Gods,

beyond believing in Messiahs or their man-made laws.

Only the sound of the night owl

penetrates my heart these moonlit hours

along the Withlacoochee this night of perfect weather;

and only a trail of swan feathers

leads me back to a love lost and found,

only to be lost forever to the hard, cold ground;

and only you, my belovèd partner long departed,

brings joy and regret to my disquieted heart;

and we, at the end of our lives,

look back with an amused shrug and a dishonest sigh

and whisper the caveat *nevermore* to the vanishing sky.

Frederick Kirwin

We took a walk at sunrise along the seashore

to a place where the sea oats grow at the water's roar

and sat in the sand and sang no songs

and said no words of sun and comfort all day long.

Silence was enough—until we were older

and needed more, more than each other's shoulders;

and now we sing songs but not for each other's ears

and say no words of sun and comfort for the other to hear;

and I recall those days on the river we strolled along,

and yearn for the Withlacoochee with its old lost songs.

Frederick Kirwin

I took a walk late into the night

along the path of easy pleasure and filtering moonlight

until not only did I find pleasure and manhood

but also love amongst the Cottonwoods

that grew alongside the graveled walkway;

and what I learned is that our years, months, and days

move faster than we can recall

but that love moves fastest of all,

for when we emerged from that path of no-turning-back,

love had vanished before us, having moved faster

than the hours we had lain together

beneath the Cottonwoods amongst the dahlias and asters.

Frederick Kirwin

Shall we extinguish old flames

and never let them burn brightly again?

Should old lovers be forgotten and gotten rid of,

and should you, my brightest burning love

from a distant bed in a time now only dreamt of,

be remembered in a lovesong or remain a tale untold?

Oh, do not dwell on that Garden of Old,

my aging soul,

for the past was what it still is

and no poem can efface, nor time erase, one hour of it.

Frederick Kirwin

I hear your name in the summer wind

billowing through the Garden of Bitterroot and Chagrin

and in the breezes wafting of fennel, columbine, and rue;

and it brings joy and sadness to my heart anew,

for you are gone and the garden is but a *déjà-vu*.

Only the river remains as it widens

its way down green banks to its maritime end,

down to the omnivorous, come-hithering sea;

and I ask myself, "Is it time to leave the past?

Is it time to abandon a love singular and unsurpassed

and lose again those old lost songs of the Withlacoochee,

songs first lost so many years ago to the mythic sea?"

We were gluttons of youth, were we not, my dear,

and devoured it with delight and good cheer,

and who is to say that youth is misguided

when old age is right only about wanting to die in bed?

Frederick Kirwin

Strange, is it not, that at the end of our lives

when the Sun has been driven from our skies,

when death is as certain as the cruelty of Spring,

when life catches up to the end of all things,

that we become one with the light?

Strange, indeed, my friend, my comfort in the night,

and stranger still is my being here alone

and your body lying under a filigreed tombstone

where the Spanish Moss crowns you like a wreath of thorns

in a cemetery into which I, too, one day shall be borne

and buried, staring up into the sky forevermore.

Frederick Kirwin

This loss, this vacancy in my heart,

leaves me mourning a river on its seaward march,

and this carnal wreckage, these ravages of time and age,

leaves me less able and worldly engaged;

and these graves, this overcrowded cemetery

of old lovers, friends, and family,

lead to a tombstone awaiting me

in a bed of flowers under a live oak tree

and make my life a burdensome joy.

Still, I lift my glass of dry Apremont wine of Savoy

and toast the past with acceptance and grace

and sing those old elegiac songs for old times' sake

and for all those who have been lost and found

in the Sea of the Dying and the Drowned.

Frederick Kirwin

Your gods, those superstitions of your youth,

did not bring you long life, happiness, or truth;

and your creeds, those beliefs and caveats and rites,

did not save you in the depths of night

as you lay in the embrace of your new lover

who offered you no solace or succor,

no saints or gods or divine insights

to take you into the morning light

that broke through your window that fiery dawn

like a firebird exploding onto the scorched lawn;

and later, when you returned, abandoned and alone,

your prayers, those pleadings to the Unknown,

were heard only by me as you lay

dying in that bed of indifferent flowers on that ill-lit day

filled with the smells of death, camphor, and decay.

This heart, this roiled heart of mine,

knows no greater love in time

than the one from my youthful days of hope and desire;

and this blood, this subterranean river of fire,

rampages through old veins, frail and flaccid,

like surges over worn and dangerous rapids,

and you, my first true love from a far-off land,

have sent your heart to the Cemetery of the Damned,

and I mourn the loss of tears that cannot be shed

for the fate of all who live so briefly, then are dead

on this desolate outpost of the Gods,

this granite spinoff with its cratered façade.

Frederick Kirwin

What unhinged you so in the calm solitude

of your last night in the Earth's temperate latitudes?

What stopped you from asking of the Unknown

the meaning of life on a planet of molten rock and stone?

Was it dissatisfaction with the Deities?

Was it remembrance of old indignities?

Was it fear of the Known?

Was it fear of the Never To Be Known?

Was it fear of the unforgiving truth?

Who knows in this world of enigmatic clues?

Certainly not I on this bittersome earth

over which the Moon reigns with nocturnal rebirth

under a shroud of nightly sorrow

over a River of No Tomorrow

above a sea with its murderous undertow

and over the tombstone of the one

I loved so very long ago under the dying Sun.

Frederick Kirwin

O Belovèd, you return to me unawares

in these moments of great sadness and despair,

and I am taken back to a time in our youth

when we first were in love, a love that needed no proof;

and to this day, we remain together, though you are gone

and I am here alone, recalling you suddenly each dawn.

Frederick Kirwin

All music ends, does it not, my dear,

as do days, weeks, and passing years,

until finally all ends in the grave

regardless of how defiant are the brave

or how orchestral is the sky

or how heaven-hurled are our cries.

Frederick Kirwin

I shall sing no more those old lost songs

of the Withlacoochee one hundred fifteen miles long.

No more shall I sail the river named by the Muskogee,

down to its destination of the sea;

and never again, my dear, shall we

sing those old lost songs of love and wanderlust

and of lives long dead and turned to dust,

for life has separate rivers for all of us

and the river you sailed that wintry day

those many years ago took you far, far away

down the clear green waters that sunless Sunday

on into everlasting forgetfulness

and on into the drowning sea, deep and fathomless.

Frederick Kirwin

One day, my dear, one sunny day in May,

you will return to me in a poem of love and wordplay

in which I shall recall your resplendent face

and your guileless smile and welcoming grace

that will take me back to a Garden of Mythical Trees

and a River of Truth and a Time beyond Reach,

a splendorous time of soft summer breezes;

and, oh, that poem will be a beacon to me,

leading me to afternoons of wonder and glory,

taking me far into the Land of Memories

where we shall sail down the Withlacoochee

in search of the never-arriving sea.

Frederick Kirwin

I walk along the Paths of Pleasure down to the sea,

asking the Whisperer to whisper another word to me,

and what he whispers shall evermore be whispered by me,

for I am the Whisperer who whispers, "Nevermore,"

along the paths down to the soundless seashore.

Frederick Kirwin

I see you drifting down the Withlacoochee one torrid July,

trolling your hand into the clear, calm waters flowing by,

waters that buoyed us on into the new, alluring dawn.

I remember you, my belovèd Ghost and Companion,

as you were before the troubles began,

before the troubles began in earnest, old phantom,

before the troubles began in deepest sorrow

and ended in our parting before all our tomorrows.

Frederick Kirwin

On this night, this barren, unhappy night,

there are no more visions of you in sight,

no more memories to parse,

no more pain to be felt in my cold, inconsolate heart;

nothing—my uninspiring inspiration—

inspires me on this bitter and comfortless night,

and so I go to sleep, vacant and aimless,

hoping not to dream of ghosts, haunting and nameless.

Frederick Kirwin

We met those distant years ago at a cotillion

one Summer evening in the old Pavilion

listening to the orchestra play those joyful summer tunes

that slip out of mind like the soft, lyrical days of June,

and who knew, not I, not you, that in a few long-ago years

you would die in agony in a flowerbed, shedless of tears,

with my standing helplessly by the one I revered.

We came to a place on the river where the fish bite,

and there we dropped anchor but caught no fish all night,

for we were not anglers for fish but anglers of each other

and made love under a cool summer cloud cover

until the season ended and we were no longer one

and never again sailed the river under a soporific Sun,

seeking our chosen spot where the fish bite,

finding in each other love, faith, and delight.

Frederick Kirwin

Why sing of the dead, old friend?

Let them rest in their faraway graves at the riverbend.

Let them go on to a new life,

with new loves, betrayals, and strife.

Let them suffer anew the agonies of devotion and desire,

and let me go, dear Ghost, on to the new and inspired,

on to the truly faithful on a new day in a new sea

in a freer, kinder life with one who would never betray me.

Frederick Kirwin

Did I love you then as I love you today,

or am I still lost on a River of Never Was Anyway

and view the past through a scrim of lies and pretense?

"No matter," I say, "for comfort is in the remembrance,

and what harm is there in the truth deferred,

if truth it ever truly were?"

Frederick Kirwin

Who knows the vagaries of love?

Not you, my mourning dove,

nor I,

and certainly not they or any passerby.

Strange, is it not, not knowing

what only the Gods know

in our Garden of Phoebus Apollo?

Frederick Kirwin

A long, too long a time it has been since last I saw you;

a long, far too long a time since I lay with you anew

amongst the flowers in the soft, morning dew,

partaking of your aromas and amplitude.

It has been ages, my dear, an ageless time of unrest,

since last I held your head to my breast.

It has been an eternity, dear phantom lover,

since you left me for a grave under moss-hung cover.

And today, in an act of defiance of death,

I throw flowers of bitterness and regret

at your time-worn tombstone under a blood-red sunset.

Is that you lurking in the clouds in the darkening sky

looking at me with such despair and death in your eyes?

Or is it a vision in the night as I walk amongst the trees

looking up at the Moon and Milky Way in their infinity?

Or is it a dream of mythic coupling and romance?

Or is it a vision of Apollo singing words that enchant

the far-flung firmament with a Pythian trance?

Frederick Kirwin

Whenever I open the door, no one is there waiting for me.

Whenever I cry out your name, no one replies to my pleas

with words reassuring me that all is right.

Whenever I reach for your embrace in the middle of the night,

no arms greet me with the soft caress of a soul's delight.

And whenever I sing those old lost songs of the Withlacoochee,

I sing alone with words that no longer soothe me.

But whenever I make love in a dream on a cold winter's night,

you are there waiting for me with all your fiery appetites.

Frederick Kirwin

One day, my love, we shall dance in the Pavilion once again

along the green and fabled lake as we often did back then

where the swans cut across the water with such graceful precision,

like sailing ships of beauty in a balletic vision;

and you and I, my dear, my friend, my happiness,

will dance again the dance of forgiving forgetfulness.

Frederick Kirwin

Visions of what once was come back to haunt me,

and I call out to you tauntingly,

"Damn you for abandoning what we could have had!

Damn you for denying what we now can never have!

Damn you for not making what we had into a lifetime!

Damn you for betraying our love at its most passionate prime,

and damn you for leaving me that cruel, cursèd springtime!"

Frederick Kirwin

Shall we celebrate the past

as we lurch into the future, naked and unmasked,

hoping to find there all the glory that we had known?

Shall we sail down the river past its fallen tombstones,

unburdened of memory and regret

and create anew our history of forgive and forget?

Oh, do not reply, you who can no longer give voice to your songs,

and so I travel alone down the river as it gently rolls on

past your grave with its crumbling tombstone

and float on into the amnesial sea to ports unknown.

Frederick Kirwin

All moves on, even regrets, even betrayals, even time,

and all we have left are visions of lovemaking sublime,

visions of us in our youthful prime,

visions of what is now only a dream,

visions of the two of us on a boat trip into the unforeseen

and all the splendors in between.

Why did you return to the Garden at the end,

as you had done before, time and again?

Why did you abandon the others, the many, the lost,

lovers from the other side of the lake you'd forever crossed?

Why did you return to the place of your first love affair

and a lover you'd forsaken with a devil-may-care,

a lover you'd left behind at the Garden Gates?

Why did you return to die, destitute and intestate?

Frederick Kirwin

One day, my first true and hopeless love,

one Spring day, our youth will return in the foxgloves

strewn upon the Harlequin dance floor

where the summertime orchestra will play

with such sweet depth, necessity, and lyrical display.

Frederick Kirwin

I shall dance the dance of betrayal until my dying days

and sway to the melancholic chords of a soul at play

in the Pavilion along the Lake of Lost Splendor.

And on the Harlequin dance floor,

I will embrace my new lover with a greater love

than the love I had for you, my belovèd, betraying lover.

Frederick Kirwin

Each breath you take,

every sigh you sigh as each new day breaks,

each turn of your tantalizing body,

all of you, my dear, enthralls me,

and I close my insatiate eyes

and go to sleep with a sigh and goodbye

and dream of your young, alluring body

lying beside me under a live oak tree,

as I once again seek carnal inspiration to arouse me.

Should you, my departed lover, have fought the pain

and died raging in the blood-splattering rain?

But you did not curse death at the end.

You welcomed the inevitable that comes to all women and men

at the end of our brief rootage on this earth, dark and alien,

this blood-soaked planet hurtling into space for godless eons.

Frederick Kirwin

Should ghosts be freed from the past

and allowed to haunt the garden unabashed,

and should you and I, my phantom rose,

be allowed to wander freely in my poems and prose,

and should I, who stands guard by your graveside,

fade into the darkening night

a shadow in the diminishing light?

Frederick Kirwin

I tell myself that I do not miss you,

that you are forever banished from my view,

that the past is but a myth entrapped in a lie;

but beneath the hope lost and truth denied

is the fact that life is all the less fulfilling

without your sweet smile, deep and beguiling,

and your chiseline features and your perfect love

that returns whenever I hear the songs of a mourning dove.

I came upon your grave beneath a live oak tree

and its tombstone, solitary, lichened, and decayed,

where the Spanish Moss draped the ground

in elegiac droops hanging all around;

and there I stopped to admire the past

with its monuments to the dead long passed,

then slowly walked on and shook my head and laughed

at all our youthful hopes at long last dashed.

I lay my head upon your harboring chest

and hear a distant chord of thunder out of the West

that penetrates my soul like celestial lightning;

and I stay in your arms throughout the night,

finding there a warmth and a sanctuary

I had never known before; but you left one cold January,

though to this distant day, your remembered presence

makes my life complete and all the more pleasant,

though I am with a new love,

and you are but a phantom in the foxgloves

and in a poem of remembrance thereof.

Frederick Kirwin

I say your name over and over like an insistent tune

until it becomes a mantra to the Moon

waning in that faraway Winter of Doom;

and I cry not tears of grief for an old romance

but a lamentation of thanksgiving and acceptance

of the death of a lover cherished everlastingly,

like a requiem for the setting Moon over the Withlacoochee,

and I ask myself, not unhappily,

"Is it a joyful echo,

or is it a praiseful prayer to Apollo,

or is it a panegyric to the newer Gods,

or is it a psalm of regret for the path not trod?"

Frederick Kirwin

Why did you not speak to me that cold day in January

as you lay dying in that flowerbed under a live oak tree?

Why did you look into the distance

and lose yourself in a solitary existence?

Was it disappointment with life?

Was it disbelief in an afterlife?

Was it defiance of death?

Was it disgust with religious shibboleths?

Was it discontent with me and other lovers?

Was it despair made crueler by the winter cloud cover?

And why did you finally turn away

and bury yourself in thoughts of death and decay?

The answer, my friend,

is in our disenchantment with the Gods

and the whole, unholy, celestial fraud.

Frederick Kirwin

O Belovèd, whenever I think of you,

my hand clutches my heart anew

and touches my soul with inscrutable sorrow,

for you are gone into that endless tomorrow,

and soon I shall join you on that long, ancestral journey

singing those old lost songs of the Withlacoochee.

But we shall not grieve endlessly

for the design that the Gods have created for us,

and who but a fool would not have it thus?

Frederick Kirwin

O Belovèd, shall true love be truer still,

and shall you and I, my untrue lover of a love unfulfilled,

start over again with others and to them be truer still

and truer than you and I ever were in our untrue youths?

Oh, do not ask or play a game of gaming the truth,

for life and love and laughter are as fickle as the wind

that rids the garden of autumnal song and original sin.

Frederick Kirwin

One day, my love, we will understand this life.

One day, when we are not here to suffer its pain and strife,

we will see the world for what it is,

not as we had imagined it.

One ebullient day, one epiphanous day, I trust,

the truth will no longer be hidden from us.

One day, my belovèd soulmate and only one,

we will no longer be two but one under the Sun

when we are no longer here on this embattled earth

and are finally able to see its glory and true worth.

Frederick Kirwin

I will sing no more those old lost songs

of the river flowing gently on, quiet and strong.

I will not call out your name from our torrid past,

for the past will never return from its scattered ash.

I sing now only new songs of love and romance

with another in the Garden of Death and Deliverance.

Last Songs of the Withlacoochee

Is love later in life a slow-burning compromise

with loneliness and death and darkening skies,

a solitude burdened with the tolls of age and illness,

or is love at the end of one's earthly existence

an unexpected joy to be treasured

for its companionship, serenity, and ageless pleasures?

Frederick Kirwin

Is this the last day I will ever see you, my love?

Is this the last night we will lie as one under stars above?

Will tomorrow be the first day we are not lovers and friends

and shall never see each other again?

O true love of my latter years,

stay with me until all hope disappears

and there are no more tears

and no more Suns on the horizon

and no more Moons uprisen;

and let me be the first to depart,

for if you are not here beside me as each new day starts,

the pain would be beyond consolation

and I would roam the Garden in isolation

amongst the dying and cankered Sycamores

and sail down the crooked river nevermore.

Frederick Kirwin

Shall we sing the last songs of our lives, my love?

Shall we hold our maculated hands in well-worn gloves

as we walk down the paths of diminishing pleasure?

Shall we greet the end with a laugh and a wink for good measure,

for life has been an enigma to us

and we are lost souls on the journey from ashes to dust.

Frederick Kirwin

Is it love, you who are the better half of my whole,

or is it an accommodation of two lost souls,

or is it self-deception for the feeble and old?

"No matter," I say,

"and so what anyway,

for youth has gone the way of yesterday,

and the river has taken us far into the estuary

and we are drowning, my one and only,

in an abundance of regret and hyperbole."

Frederick Kirwin

Rest gently your head upon my weary shoulder

and stay with me on the river as we grow older,

and float with me down to the sea, the Mother of Us All,

down to the great, cradling depths in our final free fall;

and we shall sing those old last Songs of Love and Betrayal

and bury ourselves in the Necropolis of the Sea,

exultant to have arrived finally at eternity.

Frederick Kirwin

Please, true love, if old you must get,

be truer still in our final years of love and regret;

and please, please, all lovers, remain in love

despite the burdens of age and illnesses undreamt of;

and please, please, you and I,

let us be happy as we roam the Garden of Delights

with measured step and growing imbalance and failing eyesight,

and let us take each other by the arm

lest we stumble and fall into eternity alone and disarmed.

Frederick Kirwin

Shall we walk along the loud and boisterous sea

and push our way into the fog and become nonentities

before the Sun draws us back to reality?

Shall we, my dear companion amongst the dunes,

sing our final songs to the hidden stars and Moon

as we wade into the celestial waters of timeless doom?

Oh, do not ponder the end, dear soul,

for the end will soon arrive, for we are very, very old.

Frederick Kirwin

Should old songs be lost to you and me and time

and never sung again with rhythm and rhyme?

Should songs from the past

be laid to rest in the tomb of all those who've loved and passed,

and should you and I, old troubadour of the sublime,

sing our old last songs one more time

before we enter the final destination of all women and men

on this earth where we may or may not be born again?

Shall we forget the past and its glories, my dear,

we who have so little time left to play King Lear?

Shall we enter the future with nothing behind us

but ingratitude, arrogance, and old-age hubris,

for what has the past done for us

other than burden us with dreams of love and war?

Yes, to hell with all that has happened before

and three cheers to death and madness upon a misty moor!

Frederick Kirwin

Is it not strange, my dear,

that after all these years,

these happy, unembittered hours

these days amongst the embowered flowers,

these golden Autumns along the Withlacoochee,

these irrepressible Springs amidst the ferns and calla lilies,

that you and I, dear friend and belovèd other,

have found contentment—despite all the troubles—

and gained serenity amongst the forget-me-nots and hyacinths

and devotion amidst the marigolds and sweet-smelling mint?

Yes, is it not strange, comforting, and curiously exultant,

to be happy and in love and still together

as we traverse these, our last days of darkening weather?

Frederick Kirwin

We sing the last songs of love, dear comrade,

because the light no longer brightens as it had,

and the ambered dreams of innocence and youth

are cloudier and no longer seen as truth.

We sing the songs of our departure from this world,

the last songs of our lives not yet fully unfurled,

our final ballads to the Sun and Moon,

our parting farewells to these sunny afternoons,

our last goodbyes to the ever-renewing river,

our final paean to those whom we have loved and forgiven.

We sing of our satisfied lives,

our acceptance of fate in order to survive,

our final meditation in our Garden of Gethsemane,

our farewell trip down the wandering Withlacoochee.

We sing of our delight and amusement

on the paths of pleasure and contentment

and of our joy in the beds of rosemary and spearmint,

for we are still in love, or so we say,

though the Pavilion is turning into splinters of decay

and the swans swim less elegantly in the water's wake

across the green and lily-padded lake.

Yes, where to now, my old friend and journeymate?

Shall we sing our last songs to the Milky Way?

Shall we raise our voices high in our earthen hideaway?

Shall we reach truth and grandeur in the nobler spheres

and find love in our remaining days, months, and years?

O dearest love of our glorious, latter days,

stay with me unto the grave and always,

for we are no longer young and innocent and twenty-one

and our first loves have gone and returned to the Sun,

but what we have found in each other is enough.

It is enough, my dear; it is enough for us;

and, though the fire be diminished,

the needs are greater and the journey is unfinished,

and is there not truth to be discovered

on our deathbeds beneath the shrouding covers?

www.ingramcontent.com/pod-product-compliance
Lightning Source LLC
Chambersburg PA
CBHW060630130626
46555CB00002B/736